CREDO:

EXHIBITS AND OTHER POEMS

STEPHEN WIEST

CREDO:

EXHIBITS AND OTHER POEMS

STEPHEN WIEST

ODD VOLUMES

OF THE

THE FORTNIGHTLY REVIEW

LES BROUZILS

2020

Odd Volumes of
The Fortnightly Review

www.fortnightlyreview.co.uk

Editorial office:
Le Ligny
2 rue Georges Clemenceau
85260 Les Brouzils
France

ODD VOLUMES
2020

ISBN 978-0-9991365-5-3

I.

Possibilities and Perhaps

for J.A.H.

STARS *at the leap of a voice, reflect*
the mind's song, as though it were lit
by their presence, and gone echoing now
throughout the unseen worlds.
This is the tissue of generations
layering universes fragile as wave crests
showering glyphs of light,
on whatever is singular here,
elusive as songs carrying harmonics
lost from the children's morning dance
across green lawns. Remember?
Recall that game, 'Pass it on.' Recall
the prattle and reel of laughing children;
their cupped hands spilling secrets, 'Pass it on.'

That memorial may bear us on, between bells,
or through the night's collapse, whether in late April
or in our wish and memory for the world.

                        Whenever
there is a low tide leaving one beached
on morning; then, the game is simply,

'Pass it on.' And this unconcern may torture us,
rioting against the tides, inconstant
      to the moon's pull, all breath and voice.

      Beneath the summer sky, we waited for falling stars,
the bellies and baggage of our subtlety numbed.
We watched the ocean stain the beach,
the dusk becoming even darker than our blood,
hearing the surf break down the shore's long reach
as though it were outside the mind; we thought,
Perhaps it never stops for us.

      We dreamed
circles, plotting myths, moons, and masks,
moving as a twist of gnats, a slow column
on a humid afternoon, dimpling the air.

But the story passes,
or summer stops with a spiral of swans
in the evening light, a golden chain
linking the sky, the tide, the marsh.

Above the highest wing, in the sanctuary

of the evening star, the crafting of memory
begins again.

I feel, in winter's early afternoons, losses
I could never imagine in the long summer
nights of youth. How could I
ever have known the beginnings of farewells
before—that they could be so wrenching?
To pass it on is wholly without plan; this game
is wholly without anything we might consider
in the untidy baggage of our dreams.
So each new story will, with newness wasted,
urge all that would be to such renewing
as occurs each year in jonquil spring.

And so my friend, only the senile
speak of the unpromising present.
And so my friend, only the years
speak to us of what we threw away.
Nobody told us. We did not hear.
And yet, through all the voices
we would not have heard
passed a simple solemn tone:
one moment in the sequence is ours alone.

Still, the periwinkle marches
on cord-grass to the drumming moon.
Still pulsing, the surf of the imagined
contains all possibility, washing the littoral stars.

Credo: Several Exhibits

i.

We each imagine in private spaces,

In the surroundings of an invented self,

Where the electricity of these thoughts

Seems to crackle and spark in the crust

Which encasing consciousness

Images down the long nerves

Spindling through the breached walls

Of simple perspectives,

The past continues an unbreaking fever

In a blowing storm

Into this daily present

Where past and future thoughts entwine

To count and measure changes as time astounds,

Takes over, beginnings fade into forgotten

And attempt to cleanse the world once more.

ii.

Age lets loose its secrets of the heart
Sending chemistry's intricate maneuvers
Pumping hate to love and back and again,
Slowly, showing heartfelt moods
As chronic reminders of past years,
Important when they were thought to sit in days
Before inklings intruded that differences
Mirrored infinite sameness.

iii.

I watch stars, moon bright, bats on the wing,
Breezes at dusk if the moon is wan.
Even in the short darkness of high summer nights
I meander through my thoughts to the same still place,
On that mossy road to the high meadow
Where I am with the voices
Which continue to carry me through
Long days when friends look unkindly on me
Watching without connection, without substance
An image of starburst across horizons, I suppose.

iv.

All I know in daydreams of wonder,
The imagined physics of the world opens
On the beach, back to the sun, book on my lap
The tang of salt water and detritus surrounding
As the doomed red knot drifts among sanderlings

Gorging eggs after the colossal night
Of the horseshoe crabs' arrival
On the full moon in May or June
The wrack crossing life and death on the tides
A laughing gull tears the inevitable losses
All have made in the millions of journeys
From and back to the sea.

This web of the world,
That space where poems meet particles
And the continuous reckoning
With the coming moment
Displays a test of continuity of self;
A knowing—imageless, wordless, fathomless.
And the thoughts made into words
Are messengers centering the chaos in self.

V.

All I know amounts to nothing
And much of all forgotten, yet there remains
In this confusion, this fear of unknowing
Ensuing when the sun seems fragile,
And the wind sings hard songs and drops
To whisper *nothing is discoverable*, loses
A world so bright with creatures in my mind
That sometimes I think I won't come out
To be dulled by expectations of another day.

vi.

I gather myself and say yes:
I can know the reach of the mountain
The depths of each crevasse
I can consult the origin of stones,
The tectonics of plates, rumblings and fire
But the grip of comprehension
Is just behind clouds catching shapes
Around the mountain.
The nomenclature of clouds follows
Their progress and the shifting stories abound.

vii.

Though I know no God, I believe
It is not given me to know this thing,
Although I have been gifted so far counting errors,
Fewer now than those days when I knew it all.
Now I need a God who looks on an old man
Who never found the way
And who sends dragons to protect me
From consequences I never intended
And lets me see as time drifts down the hill
I climbed so long, not punishment,
Not that I did not sin, but that I struggled to praise
A swirling world with the tenacity of words.

viii.

Even thinking it from God,
The chemistry of unraveling the myth centers there
In the intricate armature of the myth's progress
In the mickle bag of stories hidden in the terroir of sleep,
Sometimes on the fertile side of the hill,
Sometimes in boggy rills where salamanders hide,
Sun startled by bright eliding circumstance
Across my eyes, and what then might appear
Glowing as something fetched whole
From my best imaginings.

ix.

I am not fearful of those who rule
From the grey shadows' world
Of their childhood discontent
Knowing I will not be separated
From the web of energy
Compelling movement in the air around me.

x.

What has been started squirms unfinished,
Twisting always into that new image,
The veined petal from a flower
Fallen from a bouquet of celebration
Peeling away a last memory
To the new one budding and a new glance coming.

xi.

Repetition flashes the key to oneself.
When clarity brings one wonder,
Its explanation brings our distinct portion
Of shame and madness
I know, having tried those voices' variety
Where meaning follows beginnings
And final images after myriad changes
Begin as pretty noises in the head,
As the sound of windchimes combines
With rain answering on the windows.

xii.

I am finding my way in age
To the center of myself, ludic,
With hints, a child's game, given
Only enough intuition to go on,
No more simple grace to believe.

Now seems the time to choose
Among the narrowing options;
For there are many remaining,
More than needed,
Often, more than wanted.

I am seeing that our theories,
Reason for no belief
So, spirit for belief in its place
Misses the target I had assumed

And the creatures living in minds
Mirrored, watching, don't know either
Holding invectives' sticks and stones
In a cracked and empty bowl.

I have come to embrace a point
Where all that I am is awash
In feelings from my last explanations
When I am as many, summer ending
In a garden where figs are fermenting
And drunken butterflies flutter in the shade.

xiii.
So, I put down words
And as I wonder
What is being said through me,
I intersperse my own phrases among those words
Words like poets yearning for a Muse
Who sometimes goes astray, becomes
As a Gypsy in my thoughts
A lump of dark origin in faded wraps
On the overlook before the city Gate
Selling bunches of lavender in a low keening whine
Where words lose their meaning,
Echoing that peculiar gypsy pain in all of us
That shouts and claps on the feet of midnight.
There is a vendor of ice cream across the road
And a *cantador* in my room of night
Announcing an Intervention and perhaps
To protect me from ruthless spinning in my words' domain.

xiv.

I read about our past, the intrigues of great ones
And wince at the pain of those lifting the stones
That empires left scattered about the world
But I don't feel that pain.
All my songs are darker now,
They tell me I have said enough,
The future has come closer,
Surrounded by now, I don't know what to do,
I have run out of gimmicks to decorate my past.

Flowing through the mediation of thought
The body aches but the mind appears translucent,
Wide empty spaces between myriad stars.

Whenever my spirit appears, I say you should be kind,
Though I am not the only one you possess,
Nor your only burden,
Yet you need me, too.
Where elsc to give or take a thought
And relive the anguish of those like me
Trying to know this extravagant place
We travel through so quickly.

xv.

Perhaps I have come too far
I relive moments as I invented them.
Wayward still and alone, keening
Fills all my elaborate systems
Despite lapses in the night's successive hours.
I am happy when the light glows and colors appear
Which each time I see amazed, again.
When clarity brings one wonder,
Its explanation brings a distinct portion
Of shame and madness.

xvi.

But it does not help, this fading darkness:
God's gone. Hordes of fat putti with him,
Carrying the bright clouds that decorated
The cerulean atop the misty landscape
Where surely His crown was forged
From the girls' smiling in old men's memories.
Then, dark clouds pass in bands,
The sun goes ghostly in grey light.
It is harder to know I will not know
Then to accept it and go on,
Turn on the light and tie my shoes.

xvii.

I see the solid pieces of the world around me
Turn abstract, a blooming mold.
Perhaps these were not visions, but mist
From too much wine, bad diet
Or the insults of love, but memory sees them
Clothed in the biases that life puts on us or we choose.

xviii.

In each mind somewhere, perhaps
In the folds of childhood, uncanny and limpid
As the air holding the wild swan's wings
Hope lingers, and sometimes stirs despite
Tolls on the road to wherever we appear
As gatekeepers reach out to settle or negotiate
Our failures and subdued responses,
These tariffs on our baggage
Hold a wind of the grace unfathomable
To have something to say to self alone
To try to make our vision's image
While whispering nothing is discoverable
My questions fall into our myths.
When I run out of wine and things to say
Then I'll dream dreams.

xix.

Even when the killing in the street evolves
From imagined rights and wrongs
Or murders in imagined times
The past continues, an unbreaking fever
Until enough is learned to accept our secrets
In this daily present
Where past and future thoughts entwine
Where Time measures change
We each imagine in private spaces,
The furnace of ideas, the relations
Of living among the living,
Investing the surrounds of an invented self,
The electricity of these thoughts
Seems to crackle and spark in the crust
Which encasing consciousness
Intertwined, something beyond
Continuous conversations, whispering
Images down the long nerves,
Spindling through the breached walls
Of simple perspectives.

I will project my thoughts on the form of a sphere
Of emptiness and let them to the wind,
Where they will sing their infinite combinations
Unless the wind wears them into itself
As grey clouds curl tops of high towers
In a blowing storm
While monsters in old men plot despite the rain.

II.

A most unaccountable obliquity

To the Beginning of Now

High tide and full moon silently sheathe
the idle thoughts I never shared,
the river is still and over the bulkhead
quiet as a monk,
and the road seems impassable
to the places we may have
only an intuition to sense

those instants feel a spirit associating
on a level tortuous to accept
but anytime might give answers all are seeking

the sere leaves rustle like thoughts arising
in the autumn of each day
from the first light of awareness
generations built from the sedimentary layers
of the mind to the images emerging
from this mish mash of dead stars

holding hands, we are seekers
but that's enough
for who can praise as I, as you,
who conjure the songs we sing

ii.
To recombine the burnt star
a long road carries stellar dust to here,
a long time to make a consciousness
flicker an instant
       what point
except to wear our time
polishing beauty and variety
in that acceleration
that immensity
bearing rainbows on the foam of consciousness

The Blue Bridge

it's a drowning creek they say
down the bend past the blue bridge
mist feeding the river
of an autumn morning
shivering in the slow voice
made of thunder and ageless
looking north toward
green water's broadening spread

a voice came with the tide
one of those times when disappointments
are held, their meetings turning bitter
and the days remembered as ink of old news
but whether from within my thoughts
or the tide's intention
the assembly of causes most times remains unknown

the ways we choose to remember the instant
the movement of the past we acted in
thinking we knew then the import of our actions
may last for weeks or disappear
as the evening sun behind a deck of clouds
as the first thunder of a summer storm

and later small parts of winter show a beauty
diminishing among the years

ii.
Who should attend this old man
standing in the doorway with his lips
turned upward in a smile
indecipherable and beguiling
I may achieve the grace of understanding myself
admitting I am that ordinary consciousness
with the twist or concern of worry that separates
the oft times of despair and abnegation

I wish for a sign from elsewhere
wondering the way each choice is made
when I need to accept that grace is here
spirit shows itself in what it has made
recedes farther on the red shift
leaves more ahead for reaching

Youth and Aging

In visions there is no time
In falling from the highest icy ledge
To appear at a lover's party without shoes
Knowing nothing about the subject
Of tomorrow's exams
Or how to find a way to the room
When the country is unknown

Renewing memories
faces of childhood smile
from the plastic telescopic views
reflecting the blue ocean of summers
we left in the attic of youth

in more thoughtful moments I wonder
if behind the eyes of imagination
it must be that muses are invented
to make the world seem sunnier
even when they say to us
heroes bloody the world for our enlightenment
or for our joy

Riddles

A glaciation might recur
with different aspects enlarged
or the cycle before
may leave no witness
or a different consciousness
more or less understanding
without anecdotes
an individual consciousness
creating history from imagination

the bias from which this history is created
by a murmur of deep time
is the creative stew that simmers where no one is

Today, A Rustling in the Shadows

Early morning brings secrets of the universe
not proven by any means at hand
to offer up to a society like this
making detailed charts of what we think
will give us some respite amid facts
that the time of the world is more than our instant of light
and deception as our mode of hope
proves a delicious folly

it may be best to leave all in early morning
for imagination's monsters are coming in daylight now
let's be wary that what we say is heard somewhere
that beauty takes pity, grants a wish
when the executioner happens by
that the cycle of commonness still plunging
toward bottom of our common means
that possibilities may become translucent
and form just beyond the last star found

and here as though on an old map
a blue corner where the unknown spawns
something beyond our ability with words
where the I *is* and images record, asking
day by day, experience by experience
how far we ride this flying horse

Remaking Clichés

I look upon a simple plodding man
Growing old remaking clichés in my long days
Sometimes thinking them brave and new
Grabbed by a spirit of my own intentions

Most times now I give up the wish to know
What it is to be a part of any of the dreams
I have searched for so long
There are so many ways my thoughts diverge
To simple mumbles, stumbling on

In the clichés of living we arrive at majesty
And the magic of acceptance, that despite
Sometimes touching an irredeemable depth,
We remain only ourselves ever changing and alone

Each time becomes more clear
In the streets wandering through the lonely pallor
Of the halogen moons, the antennae signaling silence
Of a fitful evening wrapped by the secrets of now

3 Unhappy Thoughts

1   Upside down on the wheel of fortune
Warmth all gone from the houses
The unknown territory seems empty
The black dogs are closer
The ship of fools is docked
Spreading its custom across the city

2   No one wants to live forever
everyone wants to be alive tomorrow

3   We know we do not know
the fortunate who dream know we never will.

Necessary Hope

Creativity comes from the necessary hope
That there is something of value in living,
And in celebration of this reason.
Symbols are needed, some obscure
To hide for an ambitious novice the same clichés
That reappear like buttercups and poppies each cycle.

Each story is a reading of a few late nights
Repeating into a blur of dream

I'm falling down my years now
And all the clichés are coming true
Following my interview with the world
Yet the night is dark
The only sound is rain against the shadows

Your own turn must come

I don't know where I walk in the daydream of my life
Its focus diffuses with stunning irregularity
As a limping man walking slowly out and back again into mist.

One can say this in bad times, but in better days, it is the same,
Even in the spring of a few beautiful days
There are instants when actions make complicated weather.

Where time moves inward for each aware
Of halting in their place, time for a choice
Which version of the epic belongs, which story
And which hero has adapted, and which one knows
Time is not a line, but a net, sometimes drawn up
As on a deep ocean trawler
With mermaids clinging to the sides
Singing beautiful songs of your life
Though you know
The melodies are too lovely for you alone
You fall like all the others to believing
You are exceptional and may live on and on
But sleep still escapes in those dark hours two to four
As we obsess over what is, what may be
And how to make it so.

Fragment

raging in me: anger, love—
time spent in dreaming
of desire and sometimes fear
living in a world new each day
fed from the unconscious by a dose of now
tendrils of change decorate
the rules we hold

Sweetheart have Pity

When the weariness surrounds me,
Silently holding hands with time,
I crawl out of myself
Too late to follow an understanding
To create more than a theater of better things

The scribe of my unconscious or a spirit
More ancient, knowing my yearning
Reaches deeper than some for songs,
Saying all that sing should be praised today

I have lived and watched my ignorance growing
And what should I care about a choice recombining
My many atoms as another consciousness lurking
In a body when where I have no choice or care
Everything is Here or There

On Poetry

There is a spirit who gives me truth
But takes in return my joy of making images
So, I cannot say those things I wish to celebrate
Although I know them through past sayers
Creating the poem of the vision wished
Leaves an empty sense as though stranded
In a tidal pool

I am hiding words to keep for a day
When they can be spoken
Meaning pouring out
To those in the flush of life attending
What only spirit can name

Thin the way

Hear the ospreys at twilight
When summer as always winds down
Long voyages ruffle the surface of the river

Times lived before, or thought familiar
Let us accomplish what we need of pride
But new incidents in the unfamiliar
Show how thin the way on which we walk
Shaping our history in moments
Or in their makers dreams

However, the mist will rise
A semblance of edges will appear
We crave structure because we must

From the long memory of Chaos
The world explains only the singular incidents
Consciousness needs in the bewildered present

Making myth is yesterday's science
I stand on the land
Thoughts on the waters
Dreams skyward
Among clouds always moving

Faces

Faces we talk to are aspects of Self
Creating a world with many selves mingling
When they go silent we grieve
As though a God is breathing out
The debris of his creation

We creatures of dream are riven
From our place in the swirl supporting our rise

When the I first awakens to fear of the morning
The night having caught the self
With a mask unfit for the coming day
Then immensities must be denied
Because they can't be owned
In those few steps to the walls
Containing consciousness

I am looking for that starlight
Emitted the instant I was born
Whose light will reach me tonight

When I look back across my years
Hoping the past comes to light who I am today

Physics

I try to understand the x of a second after nothing
Is this physics just another myth,
the origin understood by creativity of mythmakers
or the scientists in their different coats
each image of god lives from rituals
of the everchanging religion
origins might shuffle and dart through
the blackwater slowly moving
between trickster and other
and their clamoring iterations
choose or be responsible
or refuse and glean our misgivings
The world is made of your words
And filled out with the words of others
In the separate reality of any world
We make that explanations may follow
Words fall as pollen from the flower
a beginning and an end is imaginable
only as a question the Dream requires
God as the anonymous dreamer
Looking from the other side of creation
Through his imagination
The butterfly from nowhere
flutters up as I open my clenched fist
Above the frozen harbor

John Locke Said

In the beginning all the world was America -

Refined as in Columbus' dream
Thinking greatness needs no choirs
By those thinking to live on a gilded forever

The spirit has been draining from our ideals
For many seasons and owing to our salt and fat
We wear soft clothes and watch ourselves be entertained
Mediocrity does not astonish us.
The fault we bear is not measured or admitted.
We fragment our goings about
Slinging laws rather than holding spirit.
The old weep and the miners are dead
And gold chills the hands

As Columbus explained:
At dawn we saw naked people,
and I went ashore in the ship's boat,
armed

'collective effervescence'

To extricate myself from all these
Trinkets of Consciousness
playing loudly, with bright lights
on the edge of the familiar
the hooded spirit who chides
truth is relative to the coins on the table
for the only places monsters dwell now
are the uncharted spaces within
the elements of our imaginations
seeking new expression for ageless fears

Now they become familiar creatures
found at the edges of maps
constructing a vision from their words

Using the genealogy of dragons, the dragons
in all, to see clearly, we obfuscate
with the ability to deny out of fear
that one with the deadly glance

Standing   over there by the door

Doldrums

Imagination sees anything but everything together
Escapes in these contentious days,
I find myself amiss with feelings awry
Imagining scripts as fantastic as doubting
The world in the doldrums of my imagination

The edge of the world one's imagination touches
Is flexible in imagination's shaping,
Who can know the line where the edge
Of the world which we engage is at the edge
Of our perspective, or transported somewhere else by imagination

To celebrate the fractal sensibility of the landscape
Search the beauty that flows
Through all dimensions rather than bias
Of the individual eye by overlaying
The perspectives of a multitude of eyes

Chance

Don't blame chance; it has perspectives,
But they are not yours, they are not mine
When we confuse our questions
Perhaps the questions not asked return as answers

Our accents sometimes change meaning
In another's ear
But that everyman trying to escape
Is always there when we arrive
Ingrown pride and passing and time
Leading us to those endings
Where there are no pretty songs

ii.
Experience brings no answers to the questions
I have dragged along from a tempestuous youth

How did the myths arise except from imagination's
Desperate play   Consciousness a game
Where winning losing the competition never leaves the field

I have no more understanding than another
But passing years release demands of being right
Or handing out blame for small anxieties
I never like to hold or see others knowing that I have
As age tempers experience slowly surely to perhaps....
When the swirling silence takes shape and sound

Hic Scientia Finit....

Should you imagine an instant before creation
Has it thus been made, has it then occurred?
Simple questions cuff the sphere of understanding
To give more than other names to our own myths
Silence swirling along the boundaries of perception

We make worlds from hopes needs and fears
Tinkering with death so many generations

When I look down those swirling days
I never know the outcome of my reflection
I see only the objects I imagine
The instant before the beginning of the world
Is easy to imagine as awaking suddenly
From deep sleep and dreams dimming to forgotten
As each thing in the world hears not the I subjective
But the *I* of the life in all life
Imagining an anesthesia riding a deep breath
Awakening to the gentle inquiry of a peaceful sleep
In this moment we are the living
To the swish and swirl of a quantum perhaps…
Imagining what is and the continuing arc of its arrival

Until we meet the god we told ourselves we are,
We strive, contorting hopes as vines on ancient columns
Whose carvers had different hopes

Yet if content accepting their hopes results
Why then are we here amid our dilemmas
I only ask what everyone asks
Answers return to be deciphered as everyone's do
And different hopes deciphered from everyone's tune
I own this particular vestige of my feelings,
There is no one else in this poem
I am alone

The apostles of grace shipwreck on the rocky shore
I hear gulls and the terns cry out, but I do not recognize
The one with the feathers of light

Words

I know my mind like the edge of a woods
Changing light to shade on dead leaves
Amid vines, thorns and myriad small creatures
My words come from there
Where life slips into consciousness
Mind mirroring this universe
Words springing from mind in short bursts
In various times and most times do not say
Where they will go, what is to happen

Or give a sense of self meaningful to self
Enabling one to follow any code
Glebe from experience and learning

Change is continual
a state that knows no rest
Perspectives change at different speeds
At times outside worlds seems static
Even as we are always in our own time
Even when our own time is all of time
Sometimes I think as one from far horizons
But there is no stopping along any road
Sometimes I imagine one from afar
Has caught my thoughts, keeping most until
Time erases us all, while words may remain
even the way we hold our unchanging vistas changes
among recurring patterns

Early on a sunny morning, the mist over the field
And the river conjures images of past endeavors,
The people involved, buildings and docks all gone now
Ghosts of old stories told or imagined in this land
Where relations are intricate and never forgotten

Consciousness is not awareness
of change it is change itself
Constant not consistent
We built our biases early,
 but they didn't succor us
As we wanted more
and succumbed to greed's dissolution
but I no longer fear
instead breathe deep, celebrate
the living the past puts forth

A Scourge of Small Cords

In searching where the voices come from,
What part of thought makes them speak,
In different years changing their voice and mask
Spirit muse angel demon after many invocations
I find they are various voices of my journey
And I wonder who I was then, now changed
I will change again
The words from each experience of each face
In times meandering forward I see my past
As though I am seeing from the future
And these characters that were, I was.
I can question what my actions were
And how I might speak for them now

The paths to individual memories are various
What we need now are new maps to their meaning
What they were then is gone to the moving world
And the last time we hosted that memory
We were different and the path back to remembrance
Overgrown and prone to new memories
Some that never were some that soon may be

Oscillation

The rose and the star change in separate dimensions
Each in its measure, scale, frame
Seen by only the observer who created them

Neither chronic nor acute time is created
By those measuring that part of the cosmos
From which they snatch consciousness.

Of all the places I've lived before
in the present all were different
I slip in and out of memories
They are like the scaled translucent skin
Of the black snake shed over the loft beam
These past memories tell me where I am
different stories with differing details
Depending on where I am at the time
the same memory tells me different things
I count my gains and losses like sunshine
amid moving clouds
and these memories go outside lifetimes
Or are invented there

Let Us Begin to Sing of Younger Men

I can't escape myself enough to write
What I somehow sense to be true
I grow cold and thoughts become tentative.
Life itself is laughing in its own celebration

Age may bring that distilled experience
Becoming more concentrated more complex
Looking for additions from other perspectives

Are we really made of the dust of stars
So complex a mixture of cataclysms
And are we so grand and meaningless as this

The need to hope, to speak to something unseen
Is our best imaginations' greatest achievement
To create a divinity, to build a system of living
Then deny it and then wish it and hope it
And then die somewhere on that spectrum
Of belief and hope,
And the unknowing is how we live
Keeping us alive by asking or accepting
Until it kills us all

Conundrum

I can't keep up with my ever-changing self
That slow crumbling of aging loses importance
I strike onward to the unknown
In the conundrum of planting the field with others
Or tending one's own small patch with satisfaction
Am I now the world I would have chosen

A younger self and brighter self
May make a god from my experiences so far
The residue of all my wild dreams

Now though from the heart of my world
When the full moon rises fateful
I did not know I do not wish to know

Our world is made of words
They are the pollen in the flower
As young leaves unfurl the wind picks up
Telling them what is coming
In this hidden sense of immanence

And blinks in the course of consciousness
Are the fractals of our light saying
The inborn universe is not ours to know

Critical Edition

You are the critical edition of yourself
There is no original edition extant
because you change
whether shaping from inside
Or shaped by others passing by
Throughout your daily hopes

The critical edition is guessing
that the variant facts exist
will reassemble
a list of variables
for the next combination,
how we live
for some of the variations,
cannot be known
but seeking to make words into abstract formulas
Sufficient for a career of argument
Will not defeat the pictures falling from a stammer
And the aged man's words dissolving
Around him…

I watch the blue heron hunt in shallows
To earn patience
Watch a child become
One with generations we remember

The one sunburnt and defeated
The one bandaged but applauded
Is you, as always, everyone,
In the draughty spinning of time

And our perspectives of where we were
Will change as often as we check
the painters who thought to color heaven
With the true blue that never fades

All my teachers are dead,
all the pointers of the way are gone
I used earth's foothold to build dreams
Searching for humility's patient acceptance
of whatever one can't deal with, until one can
Or else end imitating its violence and chaos

To celebrate the splendors of the world
In the assumption that you are not of it
Will make for difficult forgiveness

We do not die rather we dissemble
The multiple lives within
May soon be left to mingle with the world
where imagination loses to despair.
The water that is me soon will be mist
The elements that make me work
may be mined again or simply forgotten
while our imaginations soar to join
the infinite stories of our world

each imagination is a spark of the world
together becoming a conflagration of spirit
weaving through the nature of a flower
and the putrefaction of corpses
on the field of yesterday's heroes

I ask myself how much I frittered away in petty causes
Insults and bile and the mediocrity of the times
not achieving the goals of self and retreating, with few changes,
back to the times I attempted to leave

I will speak to the spiders of my heart
And ask them why they spin
Across my days
Their webs leaving memories
Of who I was in silky shrouds
Swaying about me
At the window corners of the real

Journey

Epic journeys may begin from a picnic table
In a public park when the traveler is desperate
And the weather leaves no choice
They often mimic the classroom stories
Without the glitter in imagination's landscape
Coming to nothing except in the hero's mind
So, ruins of our history may give us comfort
1000 years of sun will bleach the bloods' graffiti
Our own ongoing ruins are less tidy, grey
Coated as a fall of ashes helped by rain
Everyone pays for the safety they find
The men still bind language with mockery
By sending the troubled young to killing games
practiced in rooms where the books
lie closed and the sofa empty of family
Where women will no longer weep in the shadows

these improvident variations of a theme of a man
and change so continuous it is difficult to find
the change that led to this one
perhaps there are no causes
close your eyes, imagine leaving a busy room
to consider that star outside your window
where your anxieties and your myths
may leave shadows

Grace

I try to imagine the feeling of grace
Were it given to me as an old man
Who feels the need of that state
Without trying to create it on my own
Through fear, not finding it through hope.

Sometimes I feel a spirit so close
That my blood runs cold and my hands hurt
Sometimes I feel familiar with death
A presence that does not explain
As though hearing angelic voices
Deep within a lovers' yawn

Seasons of experience orbit the rhythm of life
So understanding turns more acute
And the afternoon of simple joy might arrive
Some afternoon become tomorrow's today
With images we have never seen
To find our past in plundered tombs
To fashion tools for making myth
To entertain us or explain
From broken shards with missing words
Or on the shelves in the book of old names
of births and marriages, but mostly deaths
who was left with lands and streams
whose boundaries are lost or changed
and their worth is unremembered coinage
the food the wine the sex the love and death

the intimate aspirations and despair
in this salad of invention all lost

in a halogen brightness of a city night.

The moon, even full, is a dim reminder of another time
When thoughts floated on surprises of night
And the eyes of the hunters adjusted to darkness

This I, Vision and Dispersion

I saw the snake gliding across the tidal pool
its shadow following on the sterile sand beneath

all the grasses all the creatures
that lived and hid and hunted gone
only memories laid in disarray before our pride
a static colossus of links and chains
when things go grey in mist

Translation

The eye of a god is in the eye of all
wastrels louts and saints
who are and who will be
as the earth in satellites' eyes swirling
constant energy seeming chaotic
formal only in extremes of weather
as the depthless eyes
of cyclones gazing on oceans
our planet continues on, unaware

we live in transient global amnesia
an existential state outside of memory
asking who I am
where am I do you know what happened

forced to make songs from nothing
as talking with a child in another language
known to the child only and you amazed
at the last bright color of yesterday
between the lines of undefined emotions
when eyes contact, and vowels are sung
their stops high and low octaves mingle
when the child laughs and sings back
to you laughing

all that can be known in the brief instant
of consciousness swirling in the world's song
where every sentence reaches for an ending
and ends unsatisfied
the universe may be making images
from a strange bright point

so, drink deep from the glass filled
with the spices in unfamiliar thoughts
turning away from the collections of habit
as our baggage carves our humanity

all the deepest constructs made of air are gone
some will sparkle briefly in an off-light glow
in texts preserved for the sake of distant days
amid their displeasure and their ruins,
stones warming in the growing day,
in this place our pride has led

Another Vision

Words are on the breeze, leaves play their purpose
Begin the translation to their autumn song
I confuse songs, placed in my ears
Unable to construe their melody
My hearing filled in echoes of my shouts
At wrongs I can't control. I waste time
On the climate of sounds I will not remember
Where I ask about beginnings,
Or consciousness of the here, the now
And the difficulty imagining—
Before we were or after
These questions no longer playing
With imagination's endeavors,

These celebrations past
Hold only transition, change, now
While spending most of life in the past
Only instants are felt in the present
Sunlight on a leaf, veins tracing transparent wings
Explanations more meaningful

Than the oldest myth of creation
Conscious instants picked from the hurly burly
Beyond the first Planck epoch
Or an orange billionth of creation
We make myth, because
Our world exists, its existence completed
As images in the mind,
Completed by imagination
Through words poetry song

Constant awareness of all we will
Lose, are losing, have lost
But dawning awareness of loss
Turning less

Even bereavement may host no excuse
In all the palaces one dreams of living
The present is the crossing of the symbols
Whether we are coming from the past
Or going into the future or both
There are few which allow the door of return to open

all will record **I am**
stenciled in red ochre
palms against the wall
and words will follow
at the crossroads of chance

III.

A Vision of Perhaps

On grey days
when the world seems resting and robotic,
its infinite chores running grey and frictionless,
wheels turning hypnotic on the axle of yearning,
an absence of cause, like an idler across the room,
intrudes on yesterday's ideas, covering my ignorance
with my pride.

Like so many, running to tell half a story,
I too am everyman spinning tales
designing adventures, playing on insights
I think that I alone am privy to,
the story repeating, subtlest changes repeating,
inventing from past hurts from future dreams
all wondrous for listeners
who become as wild-eyed children at story time
along with all the strangers passing,
even though meaning might hesitate,
and I might ask why dream of wishes,
when by dreaming I wonder why
explanations seem littered by Chance,
as though with no figure no purpose
a nightingale may land on lips and sing,

words fall like numinous cabochons,
meanings cavort while I look for keys
to the places of my astonishment.

As chaos may coil the hearts of lovers
so everything possible morphs
until the whole air is full of voices
and only invisible acts call us to account

      centering each plot
in a promenade of the world's old story,
that   *What If*...   occurs before
the assertion can hold its own

looking for an explanation
with covert glances while
closing the door on the conscious,
looking directly at the action changing,
seeing truth at the corner of the eye
where light beckons to follow
to the roiled beach of imagining
where memories ride the waves
as the spume of images
drops to sand like diamonds falling

and from the dun hills beyond
the sprawling sea and the transitory beach
unknown horsemen ride out of the sunrise
many banners waving, searching a meaning
or possibly to complete some old attempt
aiming at a different ending
where heroes escape an imaginary urn
encrusted with rubies on chased gold
living their predetermined acts
gasping immortal breaths of cloud and sky,
making all glistening and new again;

as one among others I too have come
to gaze abjectly at these forlorn walls,
pushing on the curving space
of imagined action, circumspect
I nod at where I am
that what I sought is not here
especially when sitting, moving numbers
to satisfy someone's self-importance,
and while searches often fail
to comfort old and bloody truths,
at times they stomp their way
through the present hours' mediocrity
to make the day worthwhile
with thoughts swirling as storm blown skies

asking *what the…, when the…,*
and an empty basket of the present
becomes a trove of happy surprises,
no more escape for wishes to augment myths
and clothe heroes in flamboyant colors
angels and muses sing, walls become luminous
in a white room as shadows grow outward
to cover shoulders shrugging
in anticipation of another choice
surrounding that cyclical disaster
and I am sentenced for crimes
I cannot invent alone
breaking hearts, stuttering time
inventing the other as an acolyte
the riddles dance,
answers are prizes I cannot afford
whether playing or shunning the game
I want, need, to know—

Ok,

        I said Ok!
and I heard

Someone
Threw all we hold onto a midden heap
And went inside to kiss his wife or beat
His raucous children.

It's the same world
Stews to wine-bars
The tavern-keep
Tells us it is a mirage.
What does she know, fearful of attack
By the emaciated stranger at the door?
But she gives us drink, chides our quest as futile,
And tells us to be content with the long
Working day
And another by our side at night.

What else is there?

She becomes a goddess poets record, but knows it too
laughing over centuries of painful confrontations
at whomever glances back and trembles
from earlier constructs of her games,
still ringing fear out of darkness
at memories her games have scored
somewhere in porous spaces in my bones,
between the forgotten sequences in dreams…
knowing she is there always, refusing offerings
despite the great necessity she assigns them
often, I hear *endings*
endings, that's the gift
to quench the thirst of spirit—
that worth is worthless
so long as memories continue
going to nowhere and back

it's always the same denial,
this simple knowledge—
its comfort is not enough
even knowing that is not enough—

I want the knowing that is not known
   the *yes* touching the curving unknown
breaching the Beyond
to list all the limitations
even those I do not know are there.

II.

Keeping On   remains the mantra
as time subsumes all logic,
guesses too—
that's the cheville in the last word of the poem
neither arrow in time nor the arcing of its path
will explain the answerless
as all directions seem one
erratic and the same,

the intractable quiet in things

Perhaps I wish to wander on a field of stars

And this wanting light to shine for the dancing world
is where all sins hatch
only me only you, only all
take our insolvent plans
these growing symbols from our bad deeds
creating evil from a pack of wolves
imagination guiding their intricate harmonies
energy slows to words, words twist into thoughts
through the unguarded self
and all the combinations of their possibility
are merely points shining on the map of intent.

The light must be just right
the light   from the sun, moon-
light, candle, bulb, reflection from firelight,
before the image comes to fruition
not truth as some would have it
no, a *tingle* at the nape, a *shiver* only
as always, a quick tumult, words
        almost in their right order
                perhaps meaning something other,
                    who may ever know, besides
sometimes, often,   make it often, one meaning
        shines with the same light as another
                shines on the wanton's road to despair
on notes from last week's story,
expecting new paths shown by
flickering lights on intricate maps

forming images from within,
  images to form designs
to devise plot plan and compass
forms unrecognized
not present in my body's wondrous gatherings
from the touchy envelope of the day.

Just look on this angled table---
a bowl of fruit, a bee,
a ribbon of lapis lazuli
crossing the center above
a trilobite from another age
swimming in the polished Cambrian stone

Ex nihilo or *in potentia*   creation   chaos
the heresiarch is cozened
despite the celebrity of heroes
and *who is that*   I ask
imagining time's moments
here scattered through chaos
to coalesce in fleeting images.
where all the plots meet all of us.

III.

Sleep enfolds the memory of
those lost worlds
exact and indifferent to sighs and wonder,
    in adversity one dreams the best dreams----
under a layer of fear the Dream of dreams

so, I wonder when dreams seem like gifts
and waking a loss I must endure
could I make a dream with words
that stand solid as stuff of the waking world

earth, sky and wavering tides,
for in dreams the world is imagined
  unraveling the irregular spasms of time
in a single globe round me
a dream of the real world
humming about the door-stoop,

a collage of words fleshy as ripe fruit
robust and bursting, touching
that collage of words
in summers we imagine we spent,

until battered by time's hammer
and Muses laughing
the need to know is smoothed
along the hours' endless trudge
all stories metastasize
among emotions' possibilities
the dionysiac impetus to want, to achieve—
all found in the immense daybooks of loss.

When we find this *Book of Signs* it might say

the   ***SUN***

                                             and the sea

                                    rock and grass and wind
                    is

                                                    until

And the Lacunae of emptiness is everywhere

Through the rank force of desire in that emptiness
all things may grow rank as weeds in a rainy week.

The frolicking of Angels
or flights of birds,   or Muses' songs,
or senses corrupted, or merely
cycles of the flowers
          whirling too   gaudy combinations
until evening relieves that intemperate flush
with shadows on the meadow,
engaging the moment a daydream records
or evolution's slow unfolding
of all these from the aspect of the moment
painting the nerves' palette
on the wide albedo of the brain.

I never have it right, am I forced to lie?
          I know this world,
          a piece at least but words to hold it?
Words describe the pretty pictures,
but never finish smoothing each moving part.
In a day it all marches by in tiny pieces
though mostly it is night
when the full gale comes sweeping
reshuffling our odd displays
pushed down to stew a while
importuning some exit in the story's story
never losing itself.

No, hardly,
give it up and move on
until tomorrow bears its promise
though each tomorrow
also brings its tiny stain
of understanding--
having spent the days acting and dreaming
of what it might have been,
the salt and water that I am
is moving seaward.
An *ending* rests again, until another birth
will come full of blood, but joyous
where the change flowing, sometimes
presents presents
as though the spider lurks centering a thought,
the mind's web straining feelings
from the dew.

This is more than screening old clichés,
more than just a me or you;
incomplete addresses us well enough,
we stand as spirit incarnate a moment
as the dwindling flesh of us
grounds our diseases flowering over
each of us in different incarnations
until the catalog of ashes
returns with a yes.

Yes, there is no question
the axe is under the threshold
witches subdued, lightening forgone.

IV.

More often in the twilight
when colors fuse past moments
and time halts in a familiar image
something has returned here, a feeling
absorbing each wonder as a gift,
through the window a face is ghostly
a self, seen in other than a mirror,

a new projection of self in a place
chosen to reflect the self
known through the place,

beyond the pane of glass
suddenly, the back of the room is lined with books;
one makes these images in the interstices
of a life.

After dinner, staring empty
as a previous glance, the table in disarray,
empty glasses forgotten
when there is music intruding from another room,
a plaintive voice is on the phone, business can't wait
the moon plays on starlight
making shadows on a cold moment passed.

This place encircled by wishes and dreams
on the waning moon
has never gone, merely changed
on the fluctuation of moments—
eras on the axis tilting,
crusts colliding, mountains rising and falling,
plates broken, pieces carried away.

Thoughts sent into that nowhere
have not returned, but changes occur—
images, which must be spoken of,
patterns of a whole, peaceful for an instant,
before spirits invest the threshing floor,
saying choose me, winnowing seeds
from the chaff of time,

objects emptying into that Time
which holds the story touching them
clusters of stars, clusters of heartbeats,
sphere of seeds flying,
exploding nebula
White Lights in eastern breezes
corridors of the breeze
made visible by the flight
of the explosive seed heads,
or as a Bolide throwing itself to the sea
of self, seeds of the world
    and the extinction of all that childhood knew
grown into the world around the skin
that one time in the afternoon
when the sun built a road of diamonds
across the mouth of the river.

As children grow to fools   hiding
on that self-same breeze   in the agony of innocence,
among those whose assurance baffles us
and continues no matter the cycles arcing
to ask in what sense is there difference
pain is pure, present, never remembers itself
builds only its memory:

burnished breastplate chased with Medusa's head
brazen greaves and Hermes' hammered wings
showing one constrained to look for glory
decomposing in a muddy field
where seen as the trenches emptied
the wagon axles straining
under the dismembered of blast and siege
the individual gutting of the corpses of history
voices of air
compost of the unknown unremembered
who once had names various as stars.

The meanings never vary
revisions shining translucent as alabaster,
I've been here before
life spanning a story of wars and wars,
men live too long, and old men
struggling for coherence
try to live forever on the blood
of their generation's children

Once, thoughts were handled
as a phase of life, moving,
thoughts papered on walls of summer's light
it was   right for those years
when nights were shorter
time passed, and each of us
passed through time past,
to the palliative walls of recollection

laying a fine web of history over long ago,
the self each generation changes little
one to the next, I think a row of toddlers
each grasping that long line to a teacher's hand
as they are led to the playing field.

V.

Each world's a simple place itself
But so many make a loss of way through its meadows
Explaining themselves to those they meet
That sunset comes sooner, they say.

So many, yet each attempt at self
yet all the worlds, all the things
should be enough,
it is their order baffles.

Eventually, words become so heavy
they want a dream cutting
a pattern of the world
for differential tailors of philosophy
to lay them on.

Prophets shout their rage
as the reign of old thoughts recycles.
It hardly helps and then they stop for each
abruptly in different stages of woe or wonder

as these similar ambiguities
occur surrounding shaky evenings.
Now I wait for words
as the high side of night tips over
fills in words, then stops.

   I take down phrases, whole thoughts, too,
even single words and leave them
for tomorrow, for something more truthful,
something true, always incomplete;
often my thoughts in wakeful nights
seem borne along on hollow promises of tomorrow
 'The How of Worries' goads me to excess,

when everything is transformed through enchantment
to where eternity births its all-consoling myth
making each of us a wicked sorcerer
where the spirit is never reached, never seen but in flashes
when we are looking elsewhere.

So, there it is, and so

I WILL STAND OFF

Somewhere, would I say
I live by *chance* in interesting times,
or merely chaotic, and I weary and dismayed?
Chaos is the original POV.

Spirits, voices, consciousness, a random fluctuation
comes unbidden, words in my mind,
as in others', yet I eagerly save them,
they tell me things.

Age has ambiguous pleasures
those times a word won't fall
off my tongue, I taste it, know
its beginning, but its name comes
later in the day,

though sometimes words dissolve…
they hide behind each other
sometimes come together and seem
to wish respite, indiscriminate
in changing their intention without care.

Yet, my frown, my wrinkles remain—
scars of time's own laughter, they form my smile
becoming to me as my breath is welcome
when standing, facing a winter storm.

Looking inward,
I see frail bones
glitter in the sun, and my smile continues,
a gift, beyond my own assumptions.
Watch,   I raise my brow, I squint, my jaw
is tight, but then my lips relax, my smile renews
I wonder from where my words are shaped,
and what breeze has sent them.
What are we to say?
The words are minimal.
Yet they form for me, sometimes disguise themselves
—shapeshifters—turning themselves around
telling me I shall be uncluttered, too,
then, ask me what I need for happiness.

When I lower my eyelids to make a list, they laugh
as though they are old goddesses.
I smile too, but my feelings are churning anger
at laughter, as though these shapeshifters' words
want back everything I hold I am.
Sometimes, I accuse the thoughts I make,
as though they journey from far spaces
in a neuropathy of confusion.
Words in these thoughts hold shifting emotions.

When day returns, I shake a malaise
until I no longer argue with my invented smiles,
often, static for an instant,
the immanence that speaks a silent knowing,
   leaves a void, frozen
behind my eyes, yet I hear the laughter.
I must grasp answers from a sensuous world,
birds' song and their flights
in morning awakening
before the light,
all the day, and dusk
before the night
plants greening, awaiting the flower.
I am a traveler, my destination a choice of guesses,
no way presents itself,
turning in the wake of the passing known,
as a traveler finds a path
without knowing its end
or the cities along the way
to the end of the wood
back where everything I say ties itself
to the feeling of the instant
where emotions rekindle,
where the thought behind the smile
hovers on wind above the burly surf
searching the wrack on a tide-churned beach.

And I shout to all muses dancing in my dream,
Do you know me now?

Once Again

Oh my, here comes *CHANCE*   **as a wearish**
old man, become hap   hazard and contingent

A new instance becomes an old thought
as an old thought becomes a new instance
in conversation, that party perhaps
from across the room
dreams form, their flow challenges, meanings are agreed

pick one,
                    the interactions mismatched
                    the metaphors corrupt
the system seems built on irrelevant questions
reluctant answers
then it's over, we're on our way again.

VI.

Lucky me?
It remains in changing days
waiting clearing weather
to view the stars, too,
from a balcony of hope
jaded, struggling for coherence
still turning to seek vision
and prove what, a cause for the causeless?
Anyway, I've had no vision yet.

Perhaps, I must sleep in a holy place
to incubate my dreams.
Must I seek the ibis
or find the embroidered gown
and steal back the axe of knowledge and word
amid the bric a brac of sanctity?

I chase grace through sacred portals
on a bright day, still—
when I hear the door close behind me
and I ask for mercy, I find no faith.

Perhaps, it was my variation of *Chance's Song*
that gave me a melody for hope
I will not sing it for you; I am
a monotone among the singers.

It was not me but in me, is it of me,
or will hope sometimes lie
as we do to ourselves, for Chance has no stake
in our querulous natters.

Chance   the begetter of faith
when logic lies sick and leaves off
it is ourselves who take sparks from   Chance
and make them playthings in the weather of our minds.

these spin out for me
this chorus repeats
step by step the undertones diminish

   There was much more here intended,
but I went back to the
comfort of sleep,
and perhaps, there is no recall

from not attending my murmuring spirits call,
they will never forgive
and so, I may have missed it all,
been offered answers and chosen sleep.
Now, awake I know regrets that sear.

Now, I chose friends from a local world,
across the hall and down the street
and those in worlds years past
will come again to signal change
beyond the names I've called, depending on shadows
to guess their kind—voice, muse, angel,

Did you know…? Tell me!

I see the coronel of flowers in her hair
I see Santa Spirita nudging a bard,
with the spirit of the missing hand,
I see angels circling the castle,
perhaps those particles passing,
phantoms casting light on the unknown,
from the stolen flame in the fennel stalk,

the deathless essence, eidolon
whispering secrets, all these from those days
when no one crossed the sea but the sun.

Beyond the call for understanding
there has been the outward reach,

so slowly over long years,
now bowed by circumstance, I no longer
bargain with a muse in an irrevocable territory.

I have heard this wordless voice
in the off times of my self-regard
and felt its shame
in my inconstant homage to the world.

I tried to touch the laughter seen and heard,
following as faithful jester to an unhinged self
but my touch tangential all these years
until there happened in mid night suddenly,
halfway before dawn, waking from a dream forgotten
as quietly as now

a point of nothing,
dwelling somewhere here inside
I sensed it
wordless imageless
and Chance shining on its horizon
with all my accidents, their cloaks
and invisible shields falling away

For the same reasons we give to love
time and place, the opportunities
of the instant will pass
as a lover might, still hosting Hopes' stories
of further births in farther places,
in other wondrous times, where that energy is saved
but the individual signature is gone
I am part of it all along
radiating that tremulous consciousness
that point in each life--not the nameable
but the lacunae in our feelings
somewhere beyond thoughtfulness
translating only dust on meaning,   disparate
between lacunae   leaving me
only a jotter of feelings
an amanuensis of sloughed languages
written on air
yearning to be struck mute
unless my intermittent consciousness
contributes a consolation to my day,
to the grammar of a better meaning,

gives an occasion to leave the door ajar
to further budding
of all, of anything
that when not so insistent,
still faithful and unhinged

say I have felt a questing self,
standing in darkness
seen in this jester's hologram,
an infant with new, joyous reach,
Light addled Light encompassing, yes
 in this darkness
a measureless clear moment
an actual moment realizing itself
from a chrysalis to what may be

Epilogue

2020

One Spirit appeared
     Saying
The sands are building again in corners of stairways
And sliding across the garden lawns
Sands of Desolation from voices of the Prophets
Will cover the cities' towers
Even to antennae directing their aimlessness
To men's aimless motions at the harbor.

We need no Prophets now
We bind the sheaves of arrogance;
They are our reward and our inheritance,
And the ships rest, idle
     and no new harbors offer refuge,
     no country receives their cargo.

And a man stood to speak, much older
Than when he last saw the sun,
     Saying
We need no Prophets now
Despite our life of hopes and dreams,
Death remains.
As in all the years, days and eras
One Death for each.

Earth nurtures her wounds,
The sky turns blue after rain.

The sands continue to rise
In the minds of all wary,
Covering the cities walls and gates,
Filling the doorways.

We need no Prophets, we did not heed them,
They want us smaller than we have become
To raise our arms, embracing all
And within the arms' arc not to conquer
      But to be made glad,
One who questions says to Spirit,
      Why do I think of this?

We say those words which go so far beyond
We cannot follow what has caused their saying
And raw sensations become the clay
From which imagination builds worlds
Which go clear, unstoppable
Until the seventh day when the maggot drops
From the nose of the unmoving friend
And we know death abides.

Its supply must continue, broken links
Must be replaced, words must be flexible
To write a poem or say goodbye
Or decipher the text of a fortune cookie.
For those whose nights grow longer
As they walk into summer

To choose their next journey;
Time will help them
Not all end with enlightenment.

In the time of late night until the diamonds of dawn
The green briar grows across a path of the journey
So, turn the blanket to the side of blue dreams,
Accept the thorns,
The words that grow into pathways.

I will have no more prophets,
My words acquit or condemn me.

Coming like conquerors
Holding all in their homes
Without mercy to those wandering in cities
We did not know, it did not speak
Of why it came so far,
Or of wants and needs
But slew the words we held
Most precious, enslaved the rest.
We built fortresses with unkept promises
And they fell.
But we are here,
Alone in self-awareness, change
Is the future of our imagining.

Origins, beginnings, visions unfolding
Palettes of cosmic energy
Who we are, and how we
Became, from what,   wondering now

What we must do, these worrisome spill-overs
From ongoing ventures and neglects haunt us
Stumbling through our exuberant creations—

> *A spring tide on a stony beach, convulsions*
> *Of black clouds kneading thunder*
> *As lightning slices darkness roiling,*
> > *Then, the stillness of dawn, mist*
> *Hovering above the meadow,*
> > *Then, intimate flowering in the desert,*

All these worlds are listening—busy themselves
Dappling consciousness, coaxing, always anew
Come, let us dream of imaginary worlds,

> It is who we are.

Somewhere among these guesses, premises and proposals
There occurs involuntary as a spasm in a dream—

> in chills of fear, shivers of delight
> *Consciousness conjures its own Becoming,*

And from this irruption, Pride exists.
We are the center of our universe, each one,
And from Pride came an image of itself
Then, glowing from this incendiary display—
Imagination   a bawdy manipulator
And from that, my love

> *In the complex mythologies conjured*
> *Pride and Imagination, twins bound*

Came worlds and Time invented to measure them,
With an uncertainty of a second over the lifetime
Of the universe, believe, my love
From this random irruption in nothingness

We come dancing

We come dancing, my love,
shedding the dust of burnt stars
      scattering small hints
of our agony our history our unwinding,
sloughing endless explanations endless hopes
and endless pride for words closer to the deeds
unwinding through these days,
hacking through the thorny vines
we build our stories, a tower of ephemera,
the gaudier ones overcome the simple ways
we have found good but cannot love amid the glitter
which glory delegates

Together we imagine in so short direction
Never surprised to say again *all's changed,*
And if we took ice cores from the glaciers in our thought
We would find the day our blood turned warm
We moved upward on the chain we imagine
Admiring the growing epicycles of our thought
Walking backward to view the overarching reasons
All was bright enough
To start another adolescent fling
Until again the vultures gather
Circling on the grey-rimmed thermals of our deeds

Imagination *still* springs overflowing with words
carrying the baggage of our humanity
making worlds as it always has
from the   Nothingness
Behind the static across the universe
the causes in the world   the philosophies

the worships the beginnings and undoings
is imagination entertaining itself
creating this world
feelings may intertwine with others
yet an awareness rests lightly
as a shadow on a shoulder
                    Each is alone
Echoes from this loneliness send hints—
this source the radiation in each eras' myths
       a fading secondary rainbow,
all is unimaginable until its fabrication

what a world is built about each self
miming the violent clash
among the symphonies of stars
in the ongoing birth of here, now
are these thoughts forgotten
or wished for memories that never were
imagination creating its own time its own space
and yet, my love, it may not be

to those who imagine
the nearness of everything is relative
to the one who formulates it
sometimes the answers ask deeper questions
there is no forestalling the self
partaking in the dialogue of imagination with the universe
once begun is inescapable and relentless
one jots words and others appear on the page

the breeze goes slack and long shadows wish

their causal trees were gigantic too
where birds sound summing up their day
the lingering calm flows from the sun's drop
to promises of evening growing into night
call it what you will or what you must
these motes of consciousness
mostly husks and mostly bracken
fall from the air of their season
yet something settles here or there
this magic will not stop
conjuring self, shifting questions again
how quickly change has come to be everywhere
the world lived last week has fled
do you look forward, awaiting its return
how quickly rage unfurls
fear and wonder overtake the question
as a riptide pulls the beach
into its curling grasp
as unfocused images shower all

Sometimes a form indeterminate
Seeming to resemble me
Arrives from an unguarded moment
I stare into myself, part is familiar
The remaining parts of bad dreams
I never have deciphered
I don't recognize my cloak, my hood
Or what I carry, but it is radiant
A size manageable, a weight amorphous,
Changing but not overpowering
       If it lightens

It is what is left with pride diminished
Each casting off brings more clarity
Begins a sense of radiance
      If it begins to weigh
This radiance often is mistaken reflection
Tricked by our pride pretending humility
To help us hide our fears we lie
Gathering endless bits from desperate thoughts
To mix with numbers and tag them facts
It is exhausting
Everything fits together in this world
From the leaf dying, now falling
To cover the season shoring up
The endless cycle, and yet, these cycles
Have their fluctuations

One curse is to spend a lifetime pursuing what comes to be unnamed.

Suddenly the world is in flames.
The afternoon is colder than yesterday,
Daffodils are browning. The tulips shine,
Spring continues without me

As we search for where we should be forming words,
Not questions exactly
Time is burning
Every hesitant eye has brightness wiped by worry
Memories are melting like golden crowns of jasmine
The dead are bringing the gifts of their lives
To give to all an anchor to their past
Yet the song continues, a refrain repeated again

Each time as though it were the past
But, it is outside of time,
It travels with the speed of what is absolute
From flames these messengers arrive
Passing through a transparent screen
Looking back, nothing was the same
That quick flicker of consciousness in each
Forms a mirror for each to look into the world
If they so choose

About the author

Stephen Wiest, a former bartender, Fuller Brush salesman, printer, and poet-in-residence at The Johns Hopkins University, lives with his wife Susan in a small town on the Eastern Shore of Maryland. He spends his time writing, gardening and casually worrying about the world. His previous collections are Five Poems (1987) and Screeds (2013).

ODD VOLUMES

are published for subscribers to *The Fortnightly Review*.

www.fortnightlyreview.co.uk/odd-volumes/